The Livestream Blueprint

Starting and Scaling Your Business with Live Video.

JP Hightek

Perfect Zone Productions, LLC

Contents

Chapter One

Introduction

Welcome to "The Livestream Blueprint: Starting and Scaling Your Business with Live Video."

In these pages, you'll uncover the secrets of using live video to transform your business. I'm here to guide you on this exciting journey.

Why Live Video Matters:

Imagine a tool that can engage your audience like never before. That's the power of live video. It's not just about talking to a camera; it's about creating a genuine connection with your viewers. This book will show you how to harness that power for your brand's benefit.

A Step-by-Step Guide:

We'll start with the basics, understanding how

live video has shaped successful businesses. Then, we'll dive into crafting your brand identity through live streams. You'll learn how to build a community, make money, and tackle technical challenges with ease.

Your Action Plan:

Each chapter is a roadmap, packed with practical tips and real-life examples. Whether you're a beginner or an experienced livestreamer, these strategies will work for you. Think of this book as your personal mentor, providing clear advice to help you shine in the world of live video.

Why Trust Me?

I've been in your shoes, navigating the complex world of branding and media. I've seen what works and what doesn't. I was able to leverage livestreaming to scale my brand and expand my influence. Through this book, I'm sharing my expertise to help you succeed and meet your goals.

Let's Get Started: Unveiling the mask

So, grab your camera, your passion, and this book. Let's embark on this journey together. By the time you finish reading, you won't just be a livestreamer; you'll be a livestreaming expert, ready to make your mark in the digital world.

To your livestreaming success,

JP Hightek | Global Branding & Media Expert

Chapter Two

The Power of Live Video in Modern Branding

Welcome to the thrilling realm of live video, where the essence of your brand comes to life in real-time. In a digital age where screens dominate our interactions, live video offers a refreshing departure by adding a human touch to your brand story. It's not just a tool; it's a dynamic platform that allows you to engage with your audience directly, creating an immersive experience that resonates far beyond the confines of traditional marketing.

The Heart of Connection: Building Trust Through Authenticity

In the vast landscape of the internet, trust is the cornerstone of any successful business relationship. Live video is a game-changer because it lets your audience see the real people behind your brand. It's unscripted, genuine, and transparent. When you address your audience live, they witness your passion, your knowledge, and your sincerity firsthand. This authenticity fosters trust, transforming viewers into loyal customers and advocates for your brand.

Real-Life Success Stories: Inspiring Transformations

Consider the story of **Maria's Boutique**, a small online clothing store. Maria started hosting live fashion shows where she personally showcased her latest collections. Viewers not only got a front-row seat to the runway but also had the opportunity to ask questions and provide feedback in real-time. This interactive experience turned casual viewers into dedicated customers. Maria's sales skyrocketed, and her boutique gained a strong online presence, all thanks to the personal touch of live video.

In another inspiring tale, **John's Tech Tips**, a YouTube channel, started doing live product demonstrations and tech tutorials. By engaging with viewers, answering their tech queries, and even troubleshooting issues live, John transformed his channel into a tech community hub. His live sessions not only boosted his subscriber count but also led to collaborations with tech companies, turning his passion into a thriving business.

The Simplicity of Live Video: Accessible to All

Contrary to popular belief, you don't need a professional studio or a Hollywood budget to create compelling live videos. Today's smartphones are equipped with high-quality cameras, and social media platforms offer user-friendly live streaming features. It's as simple as pressing a button and connecting with your audience. Whether you're a solo entrepreneur, a small business owner, or part of a large corporation, the power of live video is within your grasp.

Pioneering the Future: Embracing Innovation

As technology continues to advance, the future of live video holds even more promise. Imagine using augmented reality to let customers virtually try on your products or using interactive features that allow viewers to participate in polls and quizzes during your live sessions. These innovations not only enhance user engagement but also create memorable experiences that leave a lasting impression.

In the chapters that follow, we will delve deeper into the strategies and techniques that can elevate your live video presence. From crafting compelling content to mastering the art of audience interaction, we'll explore every facet of live video branding. So, get ready to embark on a journey that will transform your brand, captivate your audience, and position your business at the forefront of modern branding. The stage is set, and the spotlight is on you. Let's make your brand shine brighter than ever before!

Additional Resource (Visit the link or scan the QR Code)

Growing Your Business with Live Video: https://spoti.fi/48GYjiF

Chapter Three

Crafting Your Livestream Brand Identity

Crafting a brand identity for your livestream is akin to creating a warm, welcoming hug for your audience. It's not just about visuals; it's about the essence of your brand, the core values that drive your content, and the genuine connection you establish with your viewers.

Embrace Your Uniqueness:

Your livestream is your canvas, and your originality is the brush that paints your brand's identity. Don't fall into the trap of imitating others too closely. Let your uniqueness shine; it's your magic wand. Consider LEGO, they don't just sell toys; they build entire imaginative worlds. Your livestream can be as creative and distinctive as their colorful bricks, capturing the hearts of your audience with your authenticity.

What Not to Do: *Avoid mimicking others. Be inspired, but let your individuality shine through.*

Share Your Core Values:

Your values are the guiding stars of your brand. Incorporate them into your livestreams, for they create deep, meaningful connections. Take inspiration from Patagonia, a brand deeply rooted in environmental activism. Livestreams about eco-friendly living align perfectly with their values, resonating profoundly with their audience. Authenticity builds trust, and trust is the cornerstone of engagement.

What Not to Do: *Don't compromise your values for temporary attention. Authenticity builds trust, which is key to engagement.*

Keep it Visually Appealing:

Visual harmony is the silent language that speaks volumes. Avoid cluttered visuals or confusing designs. Consistency in your branding is not just aesthetically pleasing; it's memorable. Look at Apple; their livestream events are sleek and minimal, reflecting their brand ethos. Simple, elegant visuals leave a lasting impression, ensuring your message isn't lost in a chaotic design.

What Not to Do: *Don't overwhelm your viewers with chaotic designs. Clarity in visuals ensures your message isn't lost.*

Practical Tips: Your Livestream Toolkit:

Invest wisely in your livestreaming tools. Simplicity and effectiveness should be your guiding principles. Complicated setups can hinder your creativity. User-friendly livestreaming tools like Ecamm Live, StreamYard, and OBS Studio empower creators without overwhelming them. Streamlining your setup enhances your focus on content and engagement.

What Not to Do: *Avoid overly complex tools that confuse you. Livestreaming should be about connection, not technical struggles.*

Livestream Branding Pitfalls to Avoid:

1. **Skip the Hard Sell:** Livestreams are conversations, not sales pitches. Engage sincerely; sales will follow naturally.

2. **Respond to Viewers:** Ignoring comments alienates your audience. Engage actively, creating a community vibe.

3. **Stay Positive:** Controversies might grab attention briefly, but they can harm your brand. Create a positive, inclusive space.

4. **Test Your Tech:** Technical glitches frustrate viewers. Test your equipment beforehand to ensure smooth streaming.

Case Study: Tanya Smith with Stream like a Boss TV – Founder of Get Noticed with Video

Tanya Smith, a live video coach and the visionary behind Get Noticed with Video, embodies the essence of impactful livestream branding. By exclusively leveraging live video, Tanya builds profound connections with her audience, expanding the reach of her business. Tanya works with coaches and course creators to amplify their voice and 'embrace their face' on video so they can stand out online, serve more people, and sell more of their services. What sets Tanya apart is her commitment to premium branding. She meticulously crafted a bridge between her livestream visuals, website offers, and social media presence. This coherence makes it effortless for her followers to identify and engage with her brand across several the digital platforms. Tanya's story serves as a testament to the power of strategic livestream branding, where authenticity meets consistency, creating a brand that resonates deeply with the audience.

Remember, your livestream is your personal stage. Be genuine, embrace your uniqueness, and interact with your audience sincerely. By steering clear of common mistakes and following these simple steps, you'll create livestreams that people not only watch but also love to engage with.

Additional Resource (Visit the link or scan the QR Code)

1- Telling Your brand story with Live video

https://bit.ly/BrandStorywithLive

2- Building Your Brand with Video: Free Master Class

https://bit.ly/CCUFreeMasterClassBrandVide o

Chapter Four

Building a Community through Live Streaming

Building a community through live streaming is like cultivating a garden. With care, attention, and the right strategies, your community can flourish and become a vibrant, supportive space for your audience. Let's dive into the art of community building in the world of live streaming.

Your livestream isn't just a broadcast; it's a gathering place, a virtual coffee shop where friends meet. Let's transform your viewers into a loyal community, fostering connections that last.

Consistent Engagement Matters

Advice: Regularity breeds familiarity. Consistent streaming schedules help your audience know when to find you. Be dependable like a favorite TV show.

Example: Think of how Twitch streamers like Pokimane or Ninja maintain consistent schedules. Their viewers anticipate their streams, making it a habit to tune in.

What Not to Do: Inconsistency can lead to audience drift. Stick to your schedule to build anticipation and trust.

Foster Two-Way Conversations

Advice: Livestreaming isn't a monologue. Interact actively. Respond to comments, ask questions, and make your viewers feel heard and valued.

Example: Look at how The Slow Mo Guys engage with their audience on YouTube. They respond to comments, building a sense of camaraderie with their viewers.

What Not to Do: Ignoring comments creates distance. Acknowledge your viewers; they are the heart of your community.

Create Interactive Experiences

Advice: Engage your community with interactive elements like polls, quizzes, and live Q&A sessions. Make them active participants, not just passive viewers.

Example: Consider how the YouTube channel Vsauce uses interactive elements. Their quizzes and polls turn passive watching into an engaging experience.

What Not to Do: Avoid one-sided broadcasts. Interactive sessions keep your viewers invested and excited.

Show Genuine Appreciation

Advice: Thank your community sincerely. Recognize long-time viewers, celebrate milestones, and make your community feel like a family.

Example: Check out how Jacksepticeye celebrates subscriber milestones. His gratitude videos and live events involve the community, making them feel integral to his success.

What Not to Do: Neglecting your community's contributions diminishes their enthusiasm. Appreciation strengthens bonds.

Cultivate a Positive Environment

Advice: Your livestream is your space. Foster positivity, respect, and inclusivity. A welcoming atmosphere encourages participation and growth.

Example: Explore how TED Talks maintain a respectful comment section. Moderation ensures discussions stay constructive and respectful.

What Not to Do: Tolerating negativity can drive away viewers. Uphold a positive atmosphere for a thriving community.

Reward Loyalty and Engagement

Advice: Acknowledge active community members. Host giveaways, exclusive Q&A sessions, or special events for your most engaged viewers. Appreciation fosters loyalty.

Example: Look at how the gaming community achieves this. Games often reward loyal players with in-game items, encouraging continuous engagement.

What Not to Do: Overlook your community's efforts. Recognition and rewards fuel enthusiasm.

Remember, your livestream community is a reflection of your brand. Nurture it, celebrate it, and watch it flourish. By actively engaging, appreciating, and respecting your audience, you're not just building a community; you're creating a home for like-minded individuals.

Chapter Five

Choosing the Perfect Niche

When diving into the world of livestreaming, selecting the right niche is key. Many beginners make the mistake of not considering the long-term potential of their choice. It's easy to jump in, but for sustainable success and financial gain, your niche matters.

Finding Your Passion and Profit

Experts often say to choose a niche you're passionate about, and for good reason. Your enthusiasm will be evident to your viewers. However, not all passions are profitable. You need a niche that combines your passion with commercial opportunity. Consider niches with high demand and money-making possibilities.

Becoming an Expert

Even if you're not an expert initially, you can

become one with dedication. Immerse yourself in your chosen niche. Learn from online resources and training courses. Your goal is to become knowledgeable enough to provide valuable content to your audience. The more you know, the more your viewers will trust you as an authority.

Once you've chosen your niche, stick with it. Don't jump between topics. Consistency builds a loyal audience. Focus on solving common problems within your niche. Identify the challenges your viewers face and offer solutions. Your ability to help people will set you apart.

Evaluating Your Competition

Competition is healthy; it indicates demand. Analyze other livestreamers in your niche. Determine what topics they cover and their follower count. Your goal is to stand out. Consider unique angles or ways to provide better content. Don't worry if your chosen niche has competition; it validates the market.

Monetizing Your Livestreams

If you're concerned about the commercial viability of your niche, don't fret. There are numerous ways to monetize your livestreams, which we'll explore in later chapters. Focus on providing value and building your audience. As your authority grows, so will your opportunities for monetization.

Remember, your success in livestreaming is not just about the niche; it's about your dedication, expertise, and ability to engage and assist your viewers effectively. Stay focused, keep learning, and your livestreaming journey will thrive.

Chapter Six

Expanding Your Reach with Audio Podcasts

Hey there! So, you're livestreaming to grow your brand, right? Well, one cool trick is turning your video livestreams into audio podcasts. It's like doubling your reach effortlessly!

Don't Forget Your Audio Audience

Here's a common mistake: people forget to structure their audio podcasts while livestreaming. When you're talking, remember that your content will be heard by both video and audio listeners. Acknowledging both sets of listeners is a fantastic way to expand your brand and show your followers some love.

A Few Tips for Your Podcast Journey

Now, you might be eager to start recording,

but hold on a sec! Planning is key. Think of it as branding your podcast persona. It's not just about a catchy name or cool cover art; it's about how you want your listeners to perceive your podcast.

Mission and Vision: Your Podcast's GPS

Before hitting the record button, define your podcast's mission and vision. The mission is what you want to achieve, and the vision is how you want your podcast to evolve. Having these in place ensures that every episode aligns perfectly with your goals.

Be Your Authentic Self

Your podcast reflects you, so just be yourself! Talk like you do in real life. Don't worry; there are no judges here. Also, come up with a catchy tagline for your podcast. Make it unique, relate it to your niche, and take your time crafting it. A great tagline can draw new listeners in.

Consistency Is Key

Your personal branding shouldn't be all over the place. Use the same branding across all your platforms – your website, Facebook, YouTube, and so on. Get some eye-catching cover art that represents your brand. If design isn't your thing, no worries! You can find talented folks to create it for you.

Why Consistency Matters

Imagine if your video podcast looking different from your audio podcast. Imagine it also looking different from your social media pages. It confuses people. Consistency helps your audience instantly recognize your content, no matter where they find it. So, keep it consistent and keep rocking your brand!

Case Study: Unveiling the Strategy Hacker® – Troy Sandidge

In the realm of business transformation, Troy Sandidge emerges as an unparalleled growth strategist, honored with numerous awards for his exceptional contributions. As a 3-time agency builder, 2-time CMO, and former global marketing director, Troy possesses a remarkable track record, having launched over 35 brands and orchestrated 3,250+ campaigns. His efforts have not only earned him recognition as a Top 100 Marketing Leader but have also resulted in generating a staggering $175 Million in revenue for clients across the globe.

What sets Troy apart is his innovative approach to brand strategy, epitomized by his creation of the acclaimed podcast, "iDigress." This Webby-nominated podcast, residing in the echelons of the Top 0.5% of podcasts worldwide, serves as a beacon of actionable insights. In each episode, delivered within a succinct 30-minute timeframe, Troy shares profound wisdom aimed at fueling the growth and scalability of businesses.

"I Digress" is more than just a podcast; it's a transformative platform featured on the prestigious HubSpot Podcast Network. Troy's dedication to providing tangible takeaways has not only earned him acclaim but has also amplified his reach, allowing him to connect with a broader audience. Through his podcast, Troy not only imparts knowledge but also transforms lives, giving his brand a stage to inspire and elevate individuals on their entrepreneurial journey.

Happy podcasting! Remember, being genuine and consistent will make your brand shine.

Chapter Seven

Monetizing Your Livestreams

Welcome to the exciting realm of monetization! Turning your passion for livestreaming into a revenue stream requires strategy, creativity, and integrity. Here's your expert guide to monetizing your livestreams while maintaining authenticity and audience trust.

Explore Diverse Monetization Avenues

Advice: Don't limit yourself. Explore various monetization options such as sponsored content, product placements, affiliate marketing, and channel memberships. Diversifying revenue streams ensures stability.

Example: Take inspiration from content creators like Linus Tech Tips. They seamlessly integrate sponsored content, maintaining viewer interest while generating revenue.

What Not to Do: Avoid relying solely on one income source. Diversification hedges risks and opens new opportunities.

Prioritize Audience Relevance

Advice: Align sponsored content with your audience's interests. Choose products or services that resonate with your viewers. Relevance enhances engagement and trust.

Example: Look at how lifestyle influencers promote products related to their niche. Their authenticity makes viewers more receptive to the promoted items.

What Not to Do: Promoting irrelevant products can erode trust. Always prioritize your audience's needs and preferences.

Disclose Transparently and Ethically

Advice: Transparency is non-negotiable. Clearly disclose sponsored content and paid partnerships. Honesty fosters trust, ensuring your audience understands your affiliations.

Example: Refer to how tech reviewers like MKBHD disclose sponsored segments. Transparent communication builds credibility and maintains authenticity.

What Not to Do: Lack of disclosure raises ethical concerns. Always be transparent about your collaborations.

Balance Monetization and Viewer Experience

Advice: Monetize thoughtfully. Ensure ads and sponsored segments don't overwhelm your content. Balance is key; maintain an enjoyable viewer experience.

Example: Consider how podcasters integrate ads seamlessly within their episodes. Listeners enjoy a smooth flow without interruptions.

What Not to Do: Excessive ads can drive away viewers. Prioritize content quality over excessive monetization.

Foster Genuine Partnerships

Advice: Choose partners who align with your values. Genuine partnerships create authentic endorsements. Work with brands that share your vision for long-term collaborations.

Example: Explore how beauty influencers collaborate with cosmetic brands. Genuine passion enhances product endorsements, resonating with viewers.

What Not to Do: Superficial partnerships lack authenticity. Prioritize meaningful collaborations over short-term gains.

Uphold Ethical Monetization Practices

Advice: Avoid clickbait, misleading promotions, or manipulative tactics. Ethical practices preserve your brand's integrity, ensuring sustained viewer trust.

Example: Analyze how reputable news outlets report stories accurately. Integrity in reporting builds credibility and audience loyalty.

What Not to Do: Unethical practices damage your reputation. Uphold high ethical standards in all your monetization efforts.

Measure Impact and Adjust Strategies

Advice: Analyze the effectiveness of monetization strategies. Track engagement, viewer feedback, and revenue generated. Adjust your approach based on data and audience response.

Example: Look at how social media platforms provide analytics. Data-driven decisions optimize your monetization efforts for maximum impact.

What Not to Do: Neglecting analytics hinders growth. Regularly assess your strategies to enhance monetization outcomes.

Case Study: The Honest YouTuber

Imagine a YouTuber passionate about tech reviews. They carefully select products aligned with their audience's interests. Transparent disclosures and engaging content foster a loyal following. By balancing monetization and viewer experience, they create a sustainable income. Ethical practices and meaningful partnerships solidify their reputation. Continuous analysis refines their strategies, ensuring long-term success.

Monetizing your livestreams is an art, not a one-size-fits-all solution. By integrating diverse revenue streams, prioritizing authenticity, and upholding ethical standards, you can transform your livestreaming passion into a thriving business. Stay true to your values, adapt to audience needs, and watch your brand prosper. Onward to a monetized and impactful livestreaming journey!

Additional Video Resources:

1- Making Money with Video

https://bit.ly/MakingMoneywithVideo

2- Making Money with Podcast

https://bit.ly/makeMoneywithPodcast

Chapter Eight

Making Money with Amazon Live

As we continue to explore various monetization options, it is important to spotlight a great solution offered by Amazon called the "Amazon Live" Influencer Program. Amazon Live provides an incredible opportunity to monetize your livestreams. However, there are specific criteria you need to meet to participate in this program. Here's what you need to know about becoming an Amazon Influencer and showcasing your livestream on their platform:

Joining the Amazon Influencer Program

First and foremost, to broadcast on Amazon Live, you must be accepted into the Amazon Influencer Program. This program is designed for individuals who can influence their audience and create engaging content. To be eligible, you must:

1. **Have an Active Social Media Presence:** You need to possess an active YouTube, Instagram, or Facebook account. These platforms serve as the foundation of your influence and allow you to connect with your audience effectively.

2. **Build a Substantial Follower Base:** Amazon typically looks for influencers with a considerable follower base, often around 20,000 followers or more. This requirement showcases your ability to reach and engage a significant audience.

3. **Engage Effectively:** Engaging with your viewers is crucial. Whether it's through Q&A sessions, responding to comments, or creating interactive content, your ability to interact adds value to the livestream experience.

4. **Relevance to Amazon Products:** Your

content should be relevant to the products sold on Amazon. If your livestreams align with the categories of products available on Amazon, it enhances the chances of your application being accepted.

Showcasing Products and Earning Commissions

Once you're accepted into the Amazon Influencer Program, you can start showcasing products during your livestreams. When viewers make qualifying purchases based on your recommendations, you earn commissions. As you talk about these products, viewers can instantly make a purchase, and you earn a commission for every sale. It's like having your own virtual shop where you curate items for your audience.

Tips for Maximizing Your Earnings

1. **Authentic Recommendations**: Your audience trusts your judgment. Be genuine in your recommendations, focusing on products you genuinely love and believe in. Authenticity sells.

2. **Interactive Engagement:** Encourage viewers to ask questions about the products you're showcasing. Answer queries live, providing valuable insights. The more engaged your audience, the higher the likelihood of sales.

3. **Creative Presentation:** Think of your livestream as a show. Use creative storytelling and demonstrations to highlight the features and benefits of the products. Engage your audience visually and intellectually.

4. **Consistent Schedule:** Establish a regular streaming schedule. Consistency builds a loyal audience, increasing the chances of repeat customers and higher commissions.

5. **Promote Your Livestream:** Leverage your social media channels and email newsletters to promote your Amazon Live sessions. The more viewers you attract, the more potential sales and earnings.

Tracking Your Earnings

Amazon provides a user-friendly dashboard where you can track your earnings, giving you insights into which products are popular among your audience. This data is invaluable, helping you refine your future streaming content for even greater success. By meeting these criteria and effectively engaging your audience, you can not only join the Amazon Influencer Program but also create a lucrative income stream through Amazon Live. So, focus on building your influence, connecting authentically with your viewers, and let your livestreams become a gateway to substantial earnings on Amazon Live!

True Success Story

Amazon Live not only offers a platform for influencers to monetize their livestreams but also provides opportunities for community building and mentorship. Let's delve into the inspiring case study of a successful Amazon Influencer, Monte Weaver, who has not only leveraged Amazon Live to grow his revenue but has also created a thriving community on Facebook called "Amazon LIVE Creators."

Case Study 1: Monte Weaver

Mastering Amazon Live and Empowering Creators

Monte Weaver is a standout Amazon Influencer who has transformed his livestreams into a profitable venture while empowering others to do the same. With a passion for authentic content creation, Monte ventured into Amazon Live, showcasing products he genuinely loved. His engaging presentations, combined with genuine product recommendations, quickly garnered a loyal audience.

Monte's Success with Amazon Live:

1. **Authentic Recommendations:** Monte's success lies in his authenticity. He carefully selects products aligning with his interests and shares genuine, enthusiastic recommendations during his livestreams. Viewers trust his judgment, leading to increased sales and commissions.

2. **Interactive Engagement:** Monte actively engages with his audience. He answers questions, demonstrates products, and provides real-time feedback, creating an immersive viewing experience. This interactive engagement fosters a sense of community, making viewers more likely to make purchases.

3. **Consistency and Promotion:** Monte maintains a consistent livestreaming schedule, allowing his audience to anticipate his broadcasts. He promotes his Amazon Live sessions across social media platforms, maximizing his reach and attracting new viewers.

Empowering Others:

Amazon LIVE Creators Community

Beyond his individual success, Monte Weaver has taken a step further by establishing the "Amazon LIVE Creators" community on Facebook. This vibrant community serves as a hub for aspiring influencers and creators looking to leverage Amazon as an income and business growth strategy.

In "Amazon LIVE Creators," Monte provides valuable insights, actionable tips, and mentorship to help members navigate the nuances of Amazon Live. The community thrives on shared experiences, collaboration, and mutual support, creating a nurturing environment for learning and growth.

Case Study 2: DealCasters

Educating and Empowering Through Expert Insights

Enter DealCasters, hosted by Jim Fuhs and Chris Stone, a beacon of education and empowerment on Amazon Live. Unlike traditional broadcasts, DealCasters goes beyond product presentations. It features insightful interviews with guest experts, exploring diverse strategies for brand expansion on Amazon Live. By spotlighting these leaders and sharing their knowledge, DealCasters empowers its audience with a wealth of actionable insights.

Unique Aspects of DealCasters:

1. **Strategic Insights:** DealCasters provides in-depth discussions on various strategies, offering viewers a comprehensive understanding of brand expansion on Amazon Live.

2. **Empowering Others:** By featuring guest experts, DealCasters equips its audience with valuable knowledge, empowering them to grow their brands effectively.

Key Takeaways :

1. **Authenticity Sells:** Authenticity and passion for products resonate with viewers, leading to increased trust and sales.

2. **Engagement Builds Community:** Interactive engagement with the audience fosters a sense of community, enhancing viewer loyalty and encouraging repeat sales.

3. **Community Empowerment:** Dedication to empowering others leads to the creation of a supportive communities where knowledge sharing and collabora-

tion drives collective success.

Monte Weaver and DealCasters exemplify the diverse approaches to success on Amazon Live. Monte thrives on authenticity and community building, while DealCasters differentiates itself through strategic insights and guest spotlights. These case studies underscore the vast opportunities Amazon Live offers—from building trust and community to providing valuable education and empowerment. As you embark on your Amazon Live journey, consider these paths to achieve your goals and empower others in the process. Remember, your unique approach can make a significant impact in the Amazon Live community.

Conclusion

Making money with Amazon Live isn't just about selling products; it's about creating an engaging, authentic experience for your viewers. By integrating the Amazon Influencer Program into your livestream strategy, you're not only monetizing your passion but also building a sustainable income stream. So, gear up, go live, and let your earnings soar as you captivate your audience on Amazon Live!

Additional Video Resources:

1- Getting Brand Deals & Growing using Amazon Live (Interview with Monte Weaver)

https://bit.ly/InterviewWithMonteWeaver

2- Making Real Money as a Full Time Influencer on Amazon Live (Interview with Chris Stone)

https://bit.ly/InterviewwithChrisStone

Chapter Nine

Technical Aspects of Livestreaming

Welcome to the technical backstage of livestreaming, where seamless broadcasts meet enthusiastic viewers. Mastering the technical aspects ensures your livestreams shine brightly, captivating your audience. Here's your expert guide to navigating the intricate world of livestreaming technology with finesse and confidence.

Investing in Quality Equipment

Advice: Quality equipment is the foundation of a flawless livestream. Invest in a high-definition camera, a reliable microphone, and professional lighting. These elements elevate your production value, leaving a lasting impression on your audience.

Example: Consider the setup of professional gamers. Their crystal-clear video and audio create an immersive experience, enhancing viewer engagement.

What Not to Do: Poor-quality equipment results in a subpar viewing experience. Don't compromise on equipment; it directly impacts your livestream's professionalism.

Choosing the Right Livestreaming Software

Livestreaming is a multifaceted art, and choosing the appropriate software is pivotal to your success. Let's explore the different levels of livestreaming and the corresponding software for each tier.

Level 1: The Selfie Livestream

At this basic level, all you need is your cell phone and an internet connection. Platforms like Facebook, Instagram, and YouTube allow you to go live directly without additional tools. Simply log in and hit "Go Live".

Level 2: Light and Microphone Upgrade

Enhance your setup with an external light

source and a microphone. These additions significantly improve the visual and audio quality of your livestream. Still, you can use your cell phone's internal livestreaming options on platforms like TikTok, Amazon Live, and Instagram.

Level 3: Browser Based Streaming

To reach this level, you'll need:

- **A Computer:** Either a laptop or desktop to access third-party livestreaming solutions.

- **External Camera:** Upgrade to a webcam or a professional mirrorless camera for better visuals.

- **External Audio:** Invest in a quality microphone. Dynamic microphones work well for live use.

- **Third Party Broadcasting Solutions:** Subscribe to web-based livestreaming platforms like Restream, Onestream Live, or Castr.

Level 4: TV Quality Production

Achieving the pinnacle of livestreaming demands additional resources:

- **A Powerful Computer**: Choose a computer with ample RAM and processing power to run professional broadcasting solutions.

- **External Professional Camera**: Opt for a camera with a clean HDMI/SDI output port, power supply compatibility, unlimited runtime, and efficient autofocus. Consider factors like output resolution, frame rate, audio pathway, and connector types.

- **Rotating Display**: Look for cameras with adjustable and rotating displays for optimal framing.

- **Portability & Size**: Consider the camera's size and portability, especially if you plan to livestream on the go.

- **Image Stabilization**: For stability during

livestreams, invest in a camera with image stabilization features.

- **Field of View:** Choose a camera with a flexible field of view to capture your preferred frame.

Recommended Cameras:

Consider cameras such as Sony mirrorless cameras (a6000, a6100, a6300, zve1, zve10), Panasonic Lumix (g7, gh4, gh5, gh5s, s5 IIX, BGH1, BS1H), and Canon mirrorless cameras (EOS R7, EOS M50 Mark II, EOS R100, R5, R50, C200, C300, C500).

Personal Recommendation:

A Level 4 broadcasting solution offers complete control over your branding elements. Consider investing in a Level 4 setup for maximum brand impact. A professional studio setup can be established for less than $15,000, ensuring a high-quality streaming experience.

Software Selection:

Experiment with software like Ecamm Live,

vMix, OBS Studio, or Wirecast, all offering powerful features with user-friendly interfaces. Many successful livestreamers prefer Ecamm Live for its customizable interface and seamless integration with various platforms.

Internet Connection:

Ensure a stable, high-speed internet connection via Ethernet to prevent lags and buffering. A seamless connection guarantees uninterrupted interaction with your viewers.

Note:

Beginners should avoid overly complex software. Start at Level 1 and gradually progress to Level 4 as your business grows. Prioritize a stable internet connection above all else to ensure a frustration-free livestreaming experience for both you and your audience. Remember, your livestreaming strategy is a key driver for business growth, and investing in the right tools can elevate your brand's online presence significantly.

Troubleshooting Common Issues

Advice: Familiarize yourself with common livestreaming issues and their solutions. Be prepared to troubleshoot problems like audio glitches, video lag, or software crashes. Quick and efficient issue resolution keeps your livestream professional and engaging.

Example: Picture a musician livestreaming a concert. If audio issues arise, knowing how to swiftly adjust settings ensures the audience enjoys a seamless musical experience.

What Not to Do: Ignoring technical glitches disrupts viewer enjoyment. Equip yourself with troubleshooting skills to handle issues promptly and maintain a high-quality livestream.

Choosing the Right Livestreaming Platform

Advice: Research livestreaming platforms to find the one aligning with your content and target audience. Platforms like YouTube Live, Twitch, and Facebook Live cater to diverse audiences. Select the platform where your content resonates the most.

Example: Cooking enthusiasts thrive on platforms like YouTube Live, where they demonstrate recipes in real-time, engaging with a food-loving audience. The platform choice enhances their content's visibility.

What Not to Do: Avoid randomly selecting a platform without understanding your audience. Each platform has unique demographics; choose one where your content finds the most receptive viewers.

Engaging with Interactive Features

Advice: Leverage interactive features like polls, live chat, and Q&A sessions. These tools create a dynamic, engaging livestream experience. Encourage viewers to participate, fostering a sense of community and connection.

Example: Think of a fitness instructor livestreaming a workout session. Interactive features allow participants to ask questions, share progress, and actively engage, enhancing the sense of a live fitness class.

What Not to Do: Neglecting interactive features diminishes viewer interaction. Actively involve your audience; their participation enriches your livestream and builds a loyal community.

Preparing for Livestreams

Advice: Plan your livestreams meticulously. Outline your content, create engaging visuals, and rehearse if necessary. A well-prepared livestream appears polished and professional, captivating your audience from start to finish.

Example: Imagine a book enthusiast hosting a livestream book review. Their slideshows, prepared talking points, and insightful commentary create a compelling, organized livestream, keeping viewers hooked.

What Not to Do: Lack of preparation leads to a disorganized livestream. Viewers appreciate well-structured content; thorough planning ensures a smooth, engaging broadcast.

Optimizing Livestream Settings for Quality

Advice: Understand the settings of your livestreaming software. Adjust video resolution, bit rate, and audio settings to achieve the best quality within your internet bandwidth limitations. Optimal settings guarantee a visually and audibly pleasing livestream.

Example: Think of a travel vlogger livestreaming from remote locations. Adjusting settings based on available internet speeds ensures viewers enjoy clear visuals and minimal buffering, despite challenging environments.

What Not to Do: Ignoring settings can lead to pixelated video or distorted audio. Familiarize yourself with your software's settings; customization elevates your livestream's professionalism.

Mastering the technical intricacies of livestreaming empowers you to create captivating, professional broadcasts. Equip yourself with quality equipment, choose the right software, maintain a stable internet connection, troubleshoot effectively, and engage with your audience using interactive features. Preparation and attention to detail ensure your livestreams leave a lasting impression, captivating viewers and fostering a dedicated community. Onward to technically flawless and engaging livestreaming experiences!

Additional Resource (Visit the link or scan the QR Code)

1- Pro Video Studio Tour https://bit.ly/TechStudioTour

2- Pro Live Video Gear Checklist https://bit.ly/ProVideoChecklist

Chapter Ten

Ownership is Key to Success

Picture this: you've poured your heart and soul into your digital creations, only to have them disappear overnight because a social media platform decided so. It's a reality check we can't ignore. In the ever-evolving realm of digital creation, where innovation meets boundless creativity, there's an essential yet often neglected principle: ownership.

Without ownership, your brand stands vulnerable, akin to building a house on shifting sands—an uncertain foundation in the turbulent digital landscape.

Understanding the Unsettling Reality

Consider the harsh realities: YouTube deleted over 100,000 videos and 17,000 channels between 2019 and 2021. In the same vein, Facebook took action against 1.3 billion accounts in Q4 2022 alone. The looming question is profound: what if these digital giants decide to erase your account one day? Will your brand endure?

The Crucial Need for Ownership

Here's the hard truth: without ownership, your brand is like a house built on shaky ground, vulnerable to being washed away by the digital tide. So, why does ownership matter? Well, it's not just about protecting your hard work; it's about increasing your brand's value. Think of it like real estate: the more you own, the more valuable your brand becomes. This means you can charge more for sponsorships and make your partnerships last longer. When you own your content and platform, you can guarantee its lifespan, a luxury you don't have on borrowed platforms like YouTube or Facebook.

Finding Your Path to Ownership: Enter Content Delivery Networks (CDNs)

Now, how do you claim this ownership? Enter Content Delivery Networks (CDNs)—your ticket to digital freedom. A reliable CDN not only shelters your videos but also lets you create your own streaming platforms, putting the power back in your hands. Among the many options out there, platforms like Ustream, RTNStreams, and Vimeo OTT stand out.

Empowering Ownership: RTNStreams.com

Consider RTNStreams.com, a game-changer in the world of CDNs. Here's what it offers:

1. **Bulletproof Video Hosting:** RTNStreams.com lets you host your videos in a secure vault, shielding them from the uncertainties of digital platforms. Your content stays yours, preserving your creative legacy.

2. **Building Your Digital Empire:** With RTNStreams.com, you can craft your own branded Roku TV or Amazon TV application effortlessly. This means more visibility and, most importantly, ownership. When you own your app, you control your brand's destiny, crucial for expand-

ing your brand's influence.

Conclusion: Cementing Your Digital Legacy

In the sprawling expanse of the digital world, ownership isn't a mere detail; it's the cornerstone upon which enduring legacies are founded. As a creator, your brand isn't just content—it's your magnum opus, your artistic fingerprint on the digital canvas. Embrace ownership, invest in a stalwart CDN like RTNStreams.com, and fortify your brand against the capricious currents of the digital ocean. Your brand's future, its timeless legacy, lies in your hands—embrace ownership, and cement your digital heritage today.

Additional Resource

Ownership and Brand Awareness:

https://bit.ly/OwnershipandBrandAwareness

Chapter Eleven

Leveraging Social Media and Marketing for Livestream Promotion

Welcome to the realm of social media mastery and strategic marketing, where your livestream gains momentum and attracts enthusiastic viewers. Promoting your livestream effectively is as essential as the content itself. In this chapter, you'll discover expert strategies to amplify your livestream's reach and engagement, building a dedicated audience eagerly awaiting your broadcasts.

Strategic Social Media Engagement

Advice: Utilize social media platforms strategically to create buzz around your livestreams. Craft engaging posts, teasers, and behind-the-scenes content to pique curiosity. Interact with your audience, responding promptly to comments and messages, building a sense of community.

Example: Think of a gaming streamer teasing an upcoming gameplay livestream on Twitter. By sharing intriguing snippets and interacting with followers' speculations, they generate excitement, ensuring a higher turnout during the actual livestream.

What Not to Do: Avoid generic, uninspired social media posts. Engage authentically; genuine interactions resonate with your audience, fostering a stronger connection and anticipation for your livestreams.

Targeted Livestream Marketing Techniques

Advice: Tailor your marketing efforts to your target audience. Identify platforms and forums frequented by your ideal viewers. Collaborate with influencers or bloggers in your niche to expand your reach. Implement targeted advertising on social media platforms to attract viewers genuinely interested in your content.

Example: Imagine a cooking enthusiast partnering with a food blogger. The blogger promotes the livestream to their food-loving audience, ensuring the content reaches individuals passionate about culinary experiences.

What Not to Do: Avoid broad, generic marketing campaigns. Specificity is key; focus your efforts where your audience resides. Targeted marketing generates higher quality leads, resulting in a more engaged livestream audience.

Engaging Livestream Announcements

Advice: Craft compelling livestream announcements. Use eye-catching visuals, intriguing captions, and countdowns to create anticipation. Incorporate interactive elements like polls or quizzes to involve your audience in the announcement, making them feel part of the event.

Example: Picture a tech expert using Instagram Stories to announce a livestream about the latest gadgets. Interactive polls asking viewers which gadget they're most excited about generate buzz and engagement before the livestream even begins.

What Not to Do: Avoid bland, uninspiring announcements. Your announcement sets the stage for viewer expectations. Make it captivating; entice your audience, leaving them eager to join your livestream.

Livestream Event Collaborations

Advice: Collaborate with other livestreamers or content creators within your niche. Joint livestream events attract both audiences, offering a unique experience. Cross-promote each other's channels, expanding your reach organically.

Example: Think of a fashion vlogger collaborating with a makeup artist for a combined livestream event. They showcase makeup techniques complementing the showcased fashion, catering to a broader audience interested in both topics.

What Not to Do: Avoid one-sided collaborations. Genuine partnerships benefit all parties involved. Ensure equal promotion and engagement, fostering a mutually beneficial relationship.

Interactive Livestream Polls and Challenges

Advice: Incorporate interactive elements like polls, challenges, or quizzes during your livestreams. Engage your viewers directly, encouraging them to participate actively. Interactive content enhances the livestream experience, creating a sense of involvement.

Example: Imagine a fitness coach conducting a livestream workout. Intermittent challenges like "Who can do the most push-ups in one minute?" involve viewers, making the livestream interactive, fun, and competitive.

What Not to Do: Avoid neglecting viewer participation. Engage with your audience; their involvement enriches the livestream, making it memorable and encouraging return viewership.

Livestream Teasers and Sneak Peeks

Advice: Create teasers and sneak peeks of your upcoming livestreams. Offer glimpses of exclusive content, special guests, or exciting activities planned. Teasers generate curiosity, motivating viewers to mark their calendars for your livestream event.

Example: Consider a musician sharing a snippet of their upcoming song performance in a livestream teaser. The captivating melody intrigues viewers, ensuring they don't miss the full performance during the livestream.

What Not to Do: Avoid vague or misleading teasers. Be genuine; your teasers should accurately represent the content viewers can expect. Authenticity builds trust, encouraging viewers to return for your future livestreams.

With strategic social media engagement, targeted marketing, engaging livestream announcements, collaborative events, interactive polls, challenges, and enticing teasers, your livestream promotion reaches new heights. Implement these expert techniques, and watch your livestream audience grow organically, creating a vibrant, engaged community eagerly anticipating your every broadcast. Onward to a thriving livestreaming journey!

Additional Audio Podcast Resource:

1- How To Develop Your Personal Branding Visibility & Engagement:

https://spoti.fi/48KH7bY

2- 5 Tips to getting more clients:

https://spoti.fi/3rKo154

Chapter Twelve

Overcoming Challenges and Growing Your Livestream Brand

Embarking on your livestreaming journey is exhilarating, yet challenges are inevitable. In this chapter, we'll explore common hurdles faced by livestreamers and equip you with expert strategies to overcome them. With a resilient mindset and strategic approach, you'll not only surmount these obstacles but also transform challenges into opportunities for unparalleled growth.

Embracing Technical Challenges

Advice: Anticipate technical issues and equip yourself with troubleshooting skills. Familiarize yourself with your equipment, software, and internet connection. Have backup solutions ready, ensuring seamless livestreams even in the face of unexpected technical glitches.

Example: Picture a gamer encountering lag during a livestream. With a backup internet connection and pre-planned intermission content, they seamlessly switch to the backup, maintaining viewer engagement until the issue is resolved.

What Not to Do: Avoid panicking in the face of technical challenges. Stay composed, swiftly implement backup plans, and communicate transparently with your audience. Authenticity during challenges strengthens your viewers' trust.

Navigating Negative Feedback and Criticism

Advice: Embrace constructive criticism as an opportunity for growth. Separate genuine feedback from trolls or malicious comments. Engage respectfully with constructive criticism, demonstrating your commitment to improving. Focus on the valuable insights to enhance your content quality.

Example: Imagine a cooking show host receiving feedback about the audio quality. They invest in a high-quality microphone, addressing the concern and significantly improving the viewer experience.

What Not to Do: Avoid dismissing feedback outright. Every critique, when dissected, holds potential for improvement. Engage thoughtfully; your willingness to evolve elevates your livestreaming brand.

Managing Content Fatigue

Advice: Maintain a consistent content schedule, but prioritize quality over quantity. Introduce variety into your livestreams, keeping your content fresh and exciting. Balance your passion projects with audience preferences, ensuring a dynamic content mix that keeps viewers engaged.

Example: Think of a fitness instructor alternating between live workout sessions, Q&A segments, and guest expert interviews. This diverse content approach caters to different viewer interests, combating content fatigue.

What Not to Do: Avoid repetitive or monotonous content. Pay attention to viewer engagement metrics; if certain content types consistently perform better, incorporate more of those into your schedule.

Strategic Collaboration and Partnerships

Advice: Collaborate strategically with influencers, experts, or fellow livestreamers. Seek partnerships aligned with your brand values and audience interests. Joint ventures introduce fresh perspectives and broaden your viewer base, enriching your livestreaming community.

Example: Imagine a technology enthusiast collaborating with a renowned gadget reviewer. Their combined livestream showcases in-depth gadget analyses and engaging discussions, captivating a broader audience fascinated by tech innovations.

What Not to Do: Avoid collaborations solely for popularity. Authenticity in partnerships resonates with viewers. Choose collaborators who genuinely align with your content, fostering meaningful, enduring connections.

Mindset Shifts for Long-Term Success

Advice: Cultivate a growth mindset. View challenges as stepping stones to improvement, not roadblocks. Embrace change, adapt to evolving trends, and continuously educate yourself. Invest in your skills and stay updated with industry advancements to remain at the forefront of livestreaming innovations.

Example: Consider a DIY crafter learning about emerging crafting techniques. By incorporating these fresh ideas into livestreams, they captivate viewers with unique, trendy projects, staying ahead of competitors.

What Not to Do: Avoid complacency. Livestreaming is a dynamic landscape; stagnation hinders growth. Embrace change, experiment with new formats, and consistently evolve your content to captivate your audience.

By navigating technical challenges, embracing feedback, combating content fatigue, fostering strategic collaborations, and maintaining a growth-oriented mindset, you're poised to overcome any obstacle on your livestreaming journey. Remember, challenges are not roadblocks but opportunities to enhance your skills, engage your audience, and elevate your livestream brand to unprecedented heights. Embrace the challenges, learn from them, and watch your livestreaming venture flourish. Onward to a resilient and thriving livestreaming future!

Additional Audio Podcast Resources:

1- Becoming More Visible "The Truth":

https://apple.co/46GmYSw

2- How To Establish your Position, Visibility and Authority:

https://apple.co/3PQaXTJ

Legal and Ethical Considerations in Livestreaming

Livestreaming offers a powerful platform to connect with your audience, but it's crucial to navigate the legal and ethical landscape responsibly. In this chapter, we'll delve into the essential considerations that ensure your livestreaming endeavors are not only engaging but also legally compliant and ethically sound. By understanding the legal nuances and upholding ethical standards, you'll safeguard your brand's reputation and create a positive, trustworthy livestreaming environment.

Understanding Copyright and Intellectual Property Rights

Advice: Respect intellectual property rights. Avoid using copyrighted material without proper authorization. Create original content or use licensed materials to prevent legal complications. Familiarize yourself with Creative Commons licenses, ensuring you comply with usage guidelines.

Example: Imagine a livestreamer incorporating background music into their stream. They use royalty-free tracks from reputable platforms, eliminating copyright concerns and providing an enjoyable viewing experience.

What Not to Do: Avoid using copyrighted images, music, or videos without permission, even if it's for a short duration. Copyright violations can lead to legal action and damage your brand's reputation.

Transparent Sponsorships and Disclosures

Advice: Be transparent about sponsored content and collaborations. Clearly disclose paid partnerships to your audience, maintaining trust. Authenticity in promotions strengthens your credibility. Use clear and visible disclaimers during sponsored segments, ensuring viewers are aware of the promotional nature.

Example: Picture a livestreamer reviewing a new gadget provided by a company. They openly disclose the collaboration at the beginning of the stream, ensuring viewers understand the context of the review.

What Not to Do: Avoid undisclosed sponsorships or vague disclosures. Transparency is key; misleading viewers erodes trust and can lead to legal repercussions.

Responsible Content Creation

Advice: Uphold ethical standards in your content. Avoid controversial or sensitive topics that could offend or harm specific communities. Research thoroughly before discussing potentially contentious subjects. Promote inclusivity and diversity, which fosters a welcoming environment for all viewers.

Example: Consider a livestreamer discussing travel experiences. They avoid culturally sensitive topics and promote respect for diverse traditions and customs, ensuring their content resonates positively with viewers from various backgrounds.

What Not to Do: Avoid inflammatory language, hate speech, or discriminatory remarks. Respectful dialogue encourages healthy discussions, while offensive content alienates viewers and tarnishes your brand image.

Protecting Viewer Privacy

Advice: Safeguard viewer privacy and data. Avoid sharing personal information about viewers without consent. Use privacy settings to protect viewer identities in live chats and interactions. Educate your audience about online privacy and encourage responsible behavior.

Example: Imagine a livestreamer moderating comments to filter out inappropriate content and protect viewer privacy. By actively managing the chat, they create a secure environment for their audience.

What Not to Do: Avoid sharing viewers' personal information, even inadvertently. Respect viewer privacy, and promptly address any privacy concerns raised by your audience.

Cultural Sensitivity and Global Audiences

Advice: Understand cultural differences when addressing a global audience. Research customs, traditions, and taboos in various regions. Exercise sensitivity in your language, visuals, and topics to avoid inadvertently offending viewers from diverse cultural backgrounds.

Example: Picture a livestreamer organizing a global cooking event. They acknowledge dietary restrictions and cultural preferences, ensuring their recipes and discussions are inclusive and respectful of diverse culinary traditions.

What Not to Do: Avoid cultural stereotypes or insensitive remarks. Respect cultural diversity, embracing the richness of global perspectives in your content.

By upholding copyright laws, maintaining transparent sponsorships, promoting responsible content creation, protecting viewer privacy, and embracing cultural sensitivity, you establish a foundation of legal and ethical integrity for your livestreaming brand. These principles not only safeguard your brand from legal issues but also cultivate a loyal, trusting audience. Uphold these standards, and your livestreaming venture will thrive, creating a positive impact while ensuring legal compliance and ethical excellence.

Additional Video Resource (Visit the link or scan the QR Code)

Protect Your Content Against DMCA Take-Down: https://bit.ly/3S0u9ke

Measuring Success: Analytics and Data-Driven Livestreaming

Understanding the metrics and data behind your livestreams is vital for optimizing your content and engaging effectively with your audience. In this chapter, we will explore key performance indicators (KPIs), analytics, and data-driven strategies to measure the success of your livestreaming efforts. By leveraging data, you can refine your content, enhance viewer engagement, and maximize the impact of your livestreams on your brand.

Identifying Key Performance Indicators (KPIs)

Advice: Define clear KPIs based on your

livestreaming goals. Whether it's viewership numbers, engagement rates, conversion rates, or audience demographics, establish metrics that align with your brand objectives. Regularly track and analyze these KPIs to measure your livestreaming success accurately.

Example: Consider a livestreamer aiming to increase product sales. Their primary KPIs include the number of viewers who click on product links during the livestream and the subsequent conversion rates. By tracking these metrics, they gauge the effectiveness of their livestreams in driving sales.

What Not to Do: Avoid overlooking KPIs or using generic metrics. Tailor your KPIs to your specific goals, ensuring you capture relevant data that provides actionable insights.

Analyzing Viewer Engagement

Advice: Monitor viewer engagement metrics such as likes, comments, shares, and average watch time. Analyze viewer comments and interactions to understand audience preferences and sentiments. Engage with your audience's feedback to foster a sense of community and make data-informed content decisions.

Example: Imagine a livestreamer analyzing viewer comments. They notice a recurring request for tutorials on specific topics. Responding to this feedback, they create dedicated livestreams, increasing viewer engagement and satisfaction.

What Not to Do: Avoid ignoring viewer feedback or dismissing engagement metrics. Viewer interactions provide valuable insights into audience preferences and content effectiveness.

Understanding Audience Demographics

Advice: Use analytics tools to gather data on your audience demographics, including age, location, gender, and interests. Understanding your audience composition helps tailor your content to meet their preferences. Analyze demographic data alongside engagement metrics to identify patterns and adapt your livestreams accordingly.

Example: Picture a livestreamer discovering that a significant portion of their audience consists of young adults interested in technology. They create livestreams focusing on the latest tech gadgets, aligning their content with their audience's interests and demographics.

What Not to Do: Avoid making assumptions about your audience demographics. Rely on data-driven insights to accurately understand your viewers, ensuring your content resonates with their interests.

Analyzing Conversion Rates and Revenue

Advice: Track conversion rates related to your livestreaming goals, such as product sales, website visits, or email sign-ups. Measure the revenue generated directly from livestreams and assess the effectiveness of your monetization strategies. Analyze the correlation between content themes and conversion rates to optimize your offerings.

Example: Consider a livestreamer promoting a limited-time discount code during their livestream. By tracking the usage of this code, they measure the conversion rate and assess the livestream's impact on sales, enabling them to refine future promotional strategies.

What Not to Do: Avoid neglecting conversion rate analysis or overlooking revenue data. Understanding the monetary impact of your livestreams is essential for assessing their overall success and refining your monetization approaches.

Utilizing A/B Testing for Content Optimization

Advice: Implement A/B testing by creating variations of your livestream content and analyzing their performance. Test different formats, topics, and presentation styles to identify what resonates best with your audience. Use the insights from A/B testing to refine your content strategy and maximize viewer engagement.

Example: Imagine a livestreamer testing two different approaches: one with interactive polls and another with in-depth product demonstrations. By comparing engagement metrics from both streams, they identify that interactive polls significantly increase viewer participation, leading to more interactive livestreams in the future.

What Not to Do: Avoid relying solely on one content format without experimentation. A/B testing provides valuable data-driven insights that can significantly enhance the effectiveness of your livestreams.

By diligently analyzing KPIs, viewer engagement, audience demographics, conversion rates, and leveraging A/B testing, you transform raw data into actionable insights. These insights empower you to refine your content, enhance audience engagement, and ultimately elevate your livestreaming brand to new heights. Embrace the power of data, and let it guide your livestreaming journey toward greater success and impact.

Chapter Fifteen

Adapting to Emerging Technologies: AR, VR, and Interactive Livestreaming

Embracing cutting-edge technologies is the key to staying ahead in the dynamic world of livestreaming. In this chapter, we will delve into the realm of augmented reality (AR), virtual reality (VR), and interactive livestreaming. By understanding and integrating these innovative technologies, you can create immersive and engaging livestream experiences that captivate your audience and set your brand apart in the competitive digital landscape.

Augmented Reality (AR) and Its Impact on Livestreaming

Advice: Explore the possibilities of AR to enhance viewer interaction and immersion during livestreams. AR overlays digital elements onto the real world, allowing for interactive graphics, animations, and special effects. Consider implementing AR elements that align with your brand identity, creating a unique and memorable livestreaming experience.

Example: Envision a beauty brand using AR filters that allow viewers to virtually try on makeup products during a livestream. This interactive experience not only engages the audience but also provides a hands-on feel of the products, boosting sales and brand loyalty.

What Not to Do: Avoid overloading your livestream with excessive AR effects that distract from your core message. Balance is key; use AR to enhance content relevance and engagement, not overshadow it.

Virtual Reality (VR) for Immersive Livestream Experiences

Advice: Explore VR livestreaming to transport viewers to virtual environments related to your brand or content. VR creates a sense of presence and immersion, allowing viewers to interact with 3D spaces and objects. Consider hosting virtual events, product launches, or behind-the-scenes tours in VR to offer an unparalleled and memorable experience.

Example: Imagine a travel agency hosting a VR livestream that virtually transports viewers to popular vacation destinations. Viewers can explore the locations in real-time, interact with tour guides, and even participate in virtual activities, creating a deep emotional connection and increasing the likelihood of booking a trip.

What Not to Do: Avoid neglecting the accessibility factor. Ensure that viewers without VR headsets can still engage with your content, either through traditional livestream platforms or interactive elements accessible via web browsers.

Interactive Livestreaming Features

Advice: Leverage interactive features such as polls, quizzes, live chats, and real-time Q&A sessions to engage viewers actively. These elements foster participation and make viewers feel directly involved in the livestream. Tailor interactive content to your audience's interests, encouraging them to share opinions, vote, and ask questions in real-time.

Example: Picture a fitness brand hosting an interactive livestream workout session. Viewers can vote on the next exercise, ask questions about proper form, and participate in live polls about their fitness goals. This interactivity not only keeps viewers engaged but also provides valuable data for future content planning.

What Not to Do: Avoid making interactivity one-sided. Encourage viewers to actively participate and respond to their contributions. Engagement should be a dialogue, not a monologue, creating a sense of community and connection.

Case Studies: Successful Implementation of AR, VR, and Interactive Livestreaming

Advice: Study real-life examples of businesses that effectively integrated AR, VR, or interactive elements into their livestreams. Analyze their strategies, audience responses, and the impact on brand perception and sales. Extract valuable lessons and consider how similar approaches could be applied to your livestreaming initiatives.

Example: Explore the case of a furniture retailer using AR to allow viewers to visualize how different pieces of furniture would look in their homes. This interactive feature significantly increased online sales as customers gained confidence in their purchasing decisions.

What Not to Do: Avoid overlooking the technical requirements and user experience. Ensure that AR, VR, or interactive elements are user-friendly, accessible, and enhance, rather than hinder, the overall livestream experience.

By embracing the immersive worlds of AR, VR, and interactive livestreaming, you elevate your content to unprecedented levels of engagement and interactivity. These technologies not only captivate your audience but also position your brand as an innovator in the digital landscape. Stay curious, experiment with these technologies, and let creativity be your guide as you craft unforgettable livestreaming experiences for your viewers.

Additional video Resource (Visit the link of scan the QR Code)

How To Leverage AI To Grow Your Business: https://bit.ly/GrowBusinessWithAI

Chapter Sixteen

Unleashing the Magic of Content Repurposing

Alright, buckle up because after your live stream extravaganza, there's a thrilling encore waiting: content repurposing! Think of it as the encore performance that keeps the audience on their feet, cheering for more. Repurposing your content isn't just a smart move; it's a game-changer for your brand. Let's dive into why and how, in a way that feels like we're having a friendly chat.

Why Content Repurposing is Your Superpower

Imagine you just hosted an epic live stream. People loved it, but not everyone could be there in the moment. Repurposing steps in to save the day!

1. Reaching Far and Wide:

You want your message to touch hearts, right? Repurposing lets you share your wisdom with a broader audience, making sure no one misses out on your brilliance.

2. Making Connections:

Different strokes for different folks, they say. Repurposing helps you connect with people in various ways. Some like videos, others prefer podcasts, and some enjoy a good read. Serve them all!

3. Climbing the SEO Ladder:

Search engines adore fresh content. When you repurpose, you create more online breadcrumbs for search engines to find you. Imagine your brand popping up in more searches – that's the magic of repurposing.

4. Establishing Authority:

Showcasing your expertise in different formats proves you're the real deal. Whether it's a snappy video, a detailed blog, or a catchy infographic, your audience sees you as the go-to person in your field.

Meet Your Sidekick: Opus Clip

Now, about making this repurposing journey a breeze – that's where Opus Clip comes in. Picture it as your trusty A.I. sidekick, a creative genius that turns your lengthy live videos into bite-sized, attention-grabbing shorts with a single click. It's like having a magical wand that transforms your content into shareable, engaging pieces.

Why Opus Clip?

- **Time Saver:** Opus Clip whizzes through your content, saving you time and effort. No need to spend hours editing; it handles the heavy lifting.

- **Quality Assurance:** Your repurposed content remains true to your live stream's essence. Opus Clip ensures your message shines through, loud and clear.

- **Engagement Booster:** Short videos are

all the rage. Opus Clip helps you create content that captures hearts, minds, and most importantly, attention.

Note: There are several other similar solutions to Opus Clip such as **2short.ai and GlossAI**. Our advice is to use any solution to help you create short videos, snippets, and reels in your content repurposing efforts.

Pro Strategies for Content Repurposing Success

1. Snackable Clips:

Slice and dice your live stream into short, engaging clips. These bite-sized wonders are perfect for social media, reeling in viewers with a taste of your awesome content.

2. Blog Bonanza:

Craft informative blogs summarizing your live stream's gems. Sprinkle in visuals, quotes, and links – your readers will love the condensed wisdom.

3. Infographic Magic:

Turn data and insights from your live stream into eye-catching infographics. People love visuals, and infographics are like candy for the eyes. Sweet, shareable, and informative.

4. Podcast Power:

If your live stream had juicy discussions, transform it into podcast episodes. Folks love tuning in while on the go, and your valuable insights will keep them coming back for more.

5. Interactive Q&A:

Host live Q&A sessions where you dive into questions related to your live stream. It's interactive, fun, and adds another layer of valuable content.

6. Email Charm:

Craft engaging email newsletters summarizing your live stream's highlights. Include links to the full video, blogs, or other repurposed gems. Emails might be old-school, but they're still gold for engagement.

In a nutshell, content repurposing isn't just a strategy; it's your brand's secret sauce. With solutions like Opus Clip as your trusty ally and these creative repurposing moves, your live stream won't just be a moment; it'll be a movement. So, embrace the magic of repurposing, and let your brand's story echo far and wide, touching lives and creating connections that last a lifetime. Cheers to your content repurposing adventure!

Lessons Learned the Easy Way

In our digital age, video content is a powerhouse for connecting with your audience and growing your brand. Live video, in particular, has become incredibly popular, creating a sense of community and engagement like never before. Let's dive into the essential lessons that will guide you in mastering live video branding, ensuring your journey is smooth and successful.

Understanding the Power of Live Video

Live video is more than just a trend; it's a genuine way to connect. The numbers don't lie—YouTube live streams have soared, highlighting the genuine appeal of live content.

When you go live, you're not just talking to an audience; you're fostering a sense of belonging. Over half of viewers feel engaged in something larger than themselves during live streams, making this a potent tool for building your brand.

Building an Engaging Brand

1. Is Your Brand Clearly Visible?

Your brand identity is your digital signature. Make sure your logo, colors, and overall identity are prominently displayed in your videos. It's vital to distinguish between your company's branding and that of your specific show. This clarity ensures your audience recognizes and remembers you.

2. Sparking Curiosity

Create a sense of wonder within your content. Pose questions, share intriguing facts, and use eye-catching visuals to keep your viewers hooked. Avoid jargon and complexity; instead, focus on sparking curiosity and keeping things simple.

3. Share Your Authentic Brand Story

Your journey matters. Share your brand's story, including the challenges you faced and how you overcame them. Authenticity builds trust and loyalty. Your audience wants to connect with real people, so be genuine and relatable.

4. Include Genuine Testimonials

Real stories from real people are incredibly compelling. Include genuine testimonials from satisfied customers or clients. These testimonials provide social proof and demonstrate the real impact your brand has had on others.

What Not to Do:

- Avoid Overcomplicating:

Don't overwhelm your audience with complex language or too much information. Keep things clear, concise, and relatable.

- Steer Clear of Inconsistency:

Inconsistency in your branding confuses your audience. Ensure your visuals, messaging, and tone remain consistent across all your videos and other brand materials.

- Don't Underestimate the Power of Engagement:

Neglecting to engage with your audience during live streams is a missed opportunity. Encourage comments, respond to questions, and make your viewers feel heard and valued.

- Avoid Being Too Formal:

While professionalism is key, don't let formality stifle your personality. Be authentic, approachable, and let your true self shine through.

Conclusion:

In the world of live video branding, simplicity and authenticity are your greatest allies. It's not just about sharing information; it's about creating connections, evoking emotions, and delivering real value. Keep it clear, keep it genuine, and remember, you're not just building a brand; you're building relationships. By following these lessons and avoiding common pitfalls, you'll craft a brand that not only captivates but also endures—a brand that resonates profoundly with your audience.

In your journey of live video branding, let these lessons be your guiding lights. Embrace simplicity, be genuine, and above all, enjoy the process of connecting with your audience in meaningful ways.

Additional Supporting material (Visit the link of scan the QR Code)

Join the Content Creators University Online School for Creators: https://bit.ly/JoinCCU

Conclusion: Unleashing the Power of Engaging Branding

In the pages of this book, we've embarked on a transformative journey through the realm of branding, media, and the art of engagement. Together, we've explored the intricacies of building not just a business, but a captivating and authentic brand that resonates with audiences across the globe.

The Essence of Engagement:

At the heart of every successful brand lies the profound ability to engage, inspire, and connect. In today's fast-paced digital landscape, where attention is fleeting and choices are abundant, the power of engagement cannot be overstated. It is the magnetic force that draws people in, keeps them enthralled, and transforms casual observers into devoted brand enthusiasts.

Authenticity as the Cornerstone:

Throughout our discussions, we've underscored the paramount importance of authenticity. Your brand's story, values, and the genuine human experiences you share are the building blocks of this authenticity. In a world inundated with artificiality, being real and relatable emerges as a beacon guiding your brand through the noise.

Embracing Technology and Innovation:

Our exploration delved into the realm of technology — the enabler of modern branding strategies. From live video streaming to immersive digital experiences, we've embraced innovative tools that amplify your brand's voice and create meaningful connections.

Fostering Community and Advocacy:

Beyond the metrics and analytics, we've discovered the essence of community. Building a loyal tribe of supporters, listeners, and customers goes far beyond transactional relationships. It embodies the creation of a shared narrative, where your brand becomes an integral part of their stories.

Your Journey Forward:

As you conclude this book, remember that the journey of branding and engagement is perpetual. It evolves, adapts, and thrives on continuous innovation. Every challenge you encounter is an opportunity to learn, grow, and refine your brand's essence.

A Heartfelt Gratitude:

I extend my deepest gratitude to you, the reader, for entrusting me with your time and attention. It has been an honor to guide you through the nuances of branding and engagement. May your endeavors be infused with authenticity, creativity, and an unwavering commitment to making a difference.

Here's to Your Engaging Brand:

As you step into the future, armed with knowledge and inspiration, I encourage you to unleash the full potential of your engaging brand. May it be a beacon of authenticity, a source of inspiration, and a catalyst for positive change.

With warmest regards,

JP Hightek | Global Branding & Media Expert

website: www.jphightek.com

Email: Connect@JPHightek.com

Your Support Matters

Dear Amazing Readers,

I hope you're having a fantastic day! I wanted to take a moment to reach out and extend my heartfelt gratitude for being such incredible supporters of my latest book. Your enthusiasm and support have meant the world to me, and I can't thank you enough for your kindness and encouragement.

Writing this book was a deeply personal journey, and your positive response has filled my heart with immense joy. Your messages, shares, and discussions about expertise have not only made my day but have also motivated me to keep working hard by writing stories that resonate with you.

Now, I have a small favor to ask. Your thoughts are incredibly important to me. Your honest reviews could make a real difference. Your words can guide fellow readers, helping them discover a book that might touch their hearts just as it touched yours.

Here's How You Can Help:

1. **Share Your Review:** If you enjoyed the book, I would be incredibly grateful if you could leave a review online. Your genuine feedback can light the way for other readers, showing them the beauty of this literary adventure.

2. **Speak Your Mind:** Your insights are priceless. Whether you loved certain parts or think there's room for improvement, your thoughts will shape my future work. Your honesty is my guiding star.

3. **Spread the Love:** If the book resonated with you, please share your experience with your friends and family. Your recommendation might just introduce the book to someone who needs its message

right now.

4. **Connect with Me**: Stay updated with my latest releases and projects by following my author page.

5. **Join the Conversation**: Follow me on various social media platforms using the handle @jphightek. Your presence in these spaces would mean the world to me.

6. **Dive into My World**: Subscribe to my YouTube channel using the same handle. Your support on this platform allows me to create more content that you might enjoy.

Your support, in whatever form it takes, fuels my passion for writing and storytelling. Together, we can create ripples of inspiration, reaching readers far and wide.

Thank you, not just for reading my book, but for being a part of this wonderful community of readers. Your support has given life to my words and purpose to my pen.

Sending you all my warmest regards and a virtual hug,

Your Fellow creator and author

JP Hightek

About The Author

As the founder of **Perfect Zone Productions**, JP Hightek has redefined the term "brand" to reach beyond business, helping individuals, entrepreneurs, organizations, and small business owners discover and embody their personal trademarked identity.

With over fifteen years' experience in the media, tech, and IT industry, JP is the the Chief Executive Officer of Perfect Zone Productions, one of the best One Stop Shop Media & Branding Agencies in the state of Tennessee.

JP has embedded his mark as an influential leader in the personal branding and creative space and was recognized and featured in several prestigious publications such as CNN, Bloomberg, ABC, NBC, Google News, Fox, Yahoo News, ESPN and many more.

JP is a Global Branding & Media Expert, a multi-talented cinematographer, software developer, Photographer, technology solutionist and the president of Reveal TV Network. His ultimate goal is to help businesses scale faster and dominate their competition.

Published by Perfect Zone Productions, LLC

A One Stop Branding & Media Agency

Website: www.PerfectZoneProductions.org

Email: Booking@PerfectZoneProductions.org

Copyright © 2023 , All Rights Reserved.